APOLLO HELMET

JAMES SCULLY

CURBSTONE PRESS   WILLIMANTIC CT

Some of these poems have appeared in
COMPAGES, HARVARD MAGAZINE, INSTEAD OF A MAGAZINE,
JUMP/CUT, MINNESOTA REVIEW, THE NEW YORKER,
THE POETRY REVIEW and THE UNREALIST

"The Soviet Union Invades Afghanistan" was published in
AND NOT SURRENDER, edited by Kamal Boullata
(Arab American Cultural Foundation, 1982)

Published with the support of the Connecticut Commission on the Arts,
a State agency whose funds are recommended by the Governor
and appropriated by the State Legislature.

We are grateful to the University of Connecticut Research Foundation
for their support.

front cover: **RAFE II** (bronze 20 x 16 x 16")
© Jeff   1972
photograph: © John Bagritsky / Jeffoto 1983

rear cover: James Scully speaking in front of
HOMBRE TRONCHADO (fired clay 45 x 55 x 20")
at the exhibition CHILE NEW YORK
on 42nd Street, May 1, 1980
photograph: © Nia Mason 1983

ISBN 0-915306-38-7 *paper*
ISBN 0-915306-39-5 *cloth*
LC 83-7269

Curbstone Press 321 Jackson St Willimantic CT 06226

APOLLO HELMET

"For it is not light that is needed, but fire. . ."

Frederick Douglass
speech at Rochester, N.Y., July 5, 1852

APOLLO HELMET

named after
the god of light, music, poetry
prophecy

conceived in the USA becoming
awful
flesh in Iran and other
colonies

is one of the simpler
special tortures

unlike tying one
to a white hot metal table,
unlike his her paralysis,

named for the god
of broad daylight

this has no features

around the victim's head
it amplifies

SCREAMS

10 times what they would be
normally

10 times
normal torture screams

after the god
also of healing
leaving no mark no scar

that's the beauty of it

the essential
message, terror
howls back
louder more familiar
sure we

hear, we heard

even without
this god of poetry
whose name will serve
any filthy thing

the way
scholars and artists
would jet to Persepolis
sucking up
oil
blood money, through
gold plated telephones
in the tent of the Shah:

with
Peter Brook playing
his 'Theatre of Cruelty'
to experts
at the Fifth Arts Festival
of Shiraz, with Ted Hughes
to come through
ORGHAST grunting

among the desert tombs
with Andy Warhol
along with so many others

the stars
whose names
escape us for the moment

along with the light, the music, poetry
the god who serves

torture, murder
you name it
any purpose

name it

AGITPROP

Principles, truth, yes but

body warmth is
winning . . .

how much humble
blood is there:
coasting and huffing
oxygen

raising
fear, pallor, blushing
not covering up

admitting
resisting
its own contradictions

flushing
depth, nuance, radi-
ance
a whole new look

like, in a less momentous
less
momentary way,
poetry.

Now this is serious
healthy attractive

persuasive.

Without this
principles
don't mean shit

FOUR-LETTER WORDS

so-called
four-letter words,
objectionable
words like 'shit'
'fuck'

like anyone else
I use them,
fragments of anger
helplessness
disgust

sometimes too they take on
weight, presence
effect: like
a slap in the face
with a two-by-four

then they're beauts,
authoritative as welts

having nothing to prove.

Mostly though
I toss them off
like broken wings
afraid disconcerted
lost

much like this woman

much the way this woman
takes running
stabs at her life:
a 'shitty' this, a
'fucking' that

showing
how tough she is
and, face it,

is not.

Is in fact
frantic, a
kitten in a sack,
hot
seed in the dark

she knows
the subways, sidewalks, cracks,
what this or that
condo or hole in Manhattan
in Brooklyn
was before that,
before that even,
better than the back
of her own hand
lumpy and cross
even so, she hasn't
been born yet, her
life seems barely
a dream
of baby fat

she
pinches herself with
words, these
crude words
to prove she's awake

wake herself

up with a foul mouth
get a reaction
get
cracking get

her ass in gear

CUNT!
PISS!

All power
to four-letter words

NATURE STUDY

Young man in a bathing suit
cool
in July swelter
signing up for the draft

he leans in
on tiptoe, his hidden arm
braced for balance
at the soft worn
edge of the counter,
his other arm
closer

holds out towards the postmaster's window
the form, signed, up over
the heads of scraggly
mostly skinny
surely, in such heat, fetid
protesters sitting and squatting
clogging the way:
too crushingly innocent
to be symbolic,
too idyllic
to scream bloody murder

the young man in the bathing suit
is graceful, courteous,
careful not to trouble them
as they are
not to stop him

it is so dis-
arming, they are
accomplices in
harmony

going off
without a ripple,
the protesters sitting
still, gawking up,
heads tilted
on necks
with the lopsided drift
of lily pads
on pond water

he eases over

dragging no shadow,
no history,
no name for the war
they will be taken with

WINNING
THE
MORAL BATTLE

losing the bloody war
the honorable few

advocate passive resistance,
go limp:

the bodies are dragged off
like dead bodies

HAVING SETTLED
FOR PERFECTION

the liberal tradition has a
deathless conception
of what
life must be like

the problem is
these others
out on a limb:
green, eager
simpleminded, they
spring to conclusions . . .

once again it is
moved to explain

to eddy
round and about, a
circumspect corpse
bound by
strips of literature,
burbling from the backwaters
of the movers and shakers
(turning soggy, corrupt
under masterpieces
metaphysics and
other
priceless junk)

telling us
all about life, but
especially life in general

PATHETIC FALLACY

And yet a camera is more
human than a penguin

this doter will ponder
weeks months in rows
the one white egg
balanced
on its broad feet

but the telephone hung up
on a desk
cord dangling
is more
moral immoral

the black and white
bundle
staggers off into spring
unable to fly, flops

tipsy and formal
into a groaning smoking sea,
plunged into

sub-feeling cold
in which
it has no need of us

is this amusing, moving

and yet
a machine a Volkswagen
beetle

a diesel rabbit whose
grandsire may have
been a gas chamber

is more human

FLAMING A

just passing through
from CA--
apocalypse kid
in baseball cap
with CAT tractor badge,
worker lookalike
except for the shorts
and poetry cassette
(his own voice
on tape) in the
dark of his pocket:

"two months ago I was at
the Rainbow Coalition, thousands
up on that hill, all high, and
you talk about unions? what shit!

peace, brother"

. . . was
the last we saw
of that

fitful and lonely

full of himself, leaving
his crap for the sweeper

POETIC DICTION

Certain words are not fit
for poetry.

Boss, for instance.
Our better verse
you may observe
has no boss in it.

The best, in fact
the most refined,
has even eliminated
jobs strikes lock-outs

not to mention unemployment.

Naturally there are no classes.
Rather, no ruling
and no working.
Just, on occasion, a middle
or an English.

It follows there is
no exploitation
no struggle
no poverty
no racist taunts
or murders, and
no injustice

because there is no
justice--

only psychology
begging questions, and
trees, menstrual blood (it's
OK it's animal nature)
with a few obscenities
classical compositions
dewy or sweaty
love, but not often

mystery, fantasy, myth
an insane asylum,
victims without victimizers
as in slabs of veal,
and a little peace . . .

there *is* peace
in poetry, the
pie in the sky
of this vocabulary

which you can bet your bottom
dollar does not include
the people with their resilience
their intelligence
seeing through
the culture police.

And this is why no one
minds
poetry anymore:

its world is one
nobody lives in, not even
poets who close their eyes
to speak

AMERICAN POETRY
AT
THE WHITE HOUSE

"   An idea that originated with board members of *POETRY* over a year ago, became a gala reality with the White House reception on January 3rd, to which Mrs. Carter invited over 500 guests for *A Salute to Poetry and American Poets.*

★

Perhaps the only dissonant
notes, heard
while we waited to enter,
were the amplified
recordings of goshawk cries
from the shrubbery
to rout
starlings from the White House lawns.

Once inside, guests were given a choice
of hearing any of several
brief poetry readings
in the handsome historic rooms
visitors generally peer
into, over
velvet museum ropes.

★

Rosalynn Carter then welcomed the guests
with a few graceful
words that thanked
the poets, for helping us to understand
our human nature.

★

The hospitality was
generous, the setting
operatic, the company
—all of us, we felt—
congenial and brilliant.

Who *was* that poet we heard
murmuring from *Childe Harold*—?

'There was a sound of revelry by night,
[The nation's] capital had gathered then
Her Beauty and her Chivalry, and bright   , ,
The lamps shone o'er fair women and brave men'

★

the above has been taken
word for word
from POETRY, March 1980
vol. cxxxv, no. 6, pp. 356-57

the poetry that did not mix
with politics

we have censored only
certain details,
we have suppressed
the role of honored names

nor will we ask
awkward questions,
not this time not

here, we will observe
a kind of decorum

★

yet let us add to this
our own good word, for

we too salute them:

we thank the poets
for helping us to understand
their human nature,
the nature of American poetry

AVANT GARDE

ahead of the game
goes up ahead
of father, mother, neighborhood,
his own generation
his class

and candid, friendly
looks around
offers his hand, says

how can you put up with this
you must get exasperated,
bored

meaning, we're the smart ones
here
the rest are clods

his look
bright and sincere
as everyone is degraded,
he himself is, you are too

as everything touched on
even in praise, turns
smaller, dirtier

under the highsounding names
of culture and art

TAKING LIBERTIES

Here it comes
quoting (sort of)
Voltaire

but Voltaire's
point was to let
misery speak, not
be tongue-tied
pieces on the rack

where was that
meaning lost?

this
one steps in: in
Greensboro Skokie
Salt Lake
City Decatur Chattanooga
Buffalo through

blood flaming crosses
firebombs,
untouched

this

ACLU
clears the way,
greases the rails
for Nazis, Klan, academic

fascists from Stanford, Berkeley, Harvard

stiff upper lip
screaming
"I may disagree
with what they say
(they? what *do* they say?)
but I'll defend to the death
their right to say it"

and 'yes' we cry, yes of course
but
whose death

whose
death did you defend
their right to

really now

REVOLVER

Cool to touch, dream
dense   he
was before he
knew it, turning
it over in his hand
oiling the cylinder
spinning it
rapid click hammer
cocked half cocked
ad-
justing trig
ger pressure
painstaking maneuver
reaming, cleaning
the barrel
bluing it, it's
warmer now, sur-
prisingly heavy
loaded

sobering, the
heft of it

he looks up, brushing
aside the litter
the tracts, leaflets, newspapers
novels
slipping it
under shirts socks
pushing shut the drawer
yes yes this

was something solid
in the soft dark,
this was
there under everything

"SOME
PULL DOWN
THE SHADES"

Some pull down the shades
and call it pacifism.

Others, the real live ones
go to prison, are raped

but neither speaks of this
or raises a hand to stop it,

not the one
nor the other

MINISTRY

So the taxpayers association
fronts for the klan, those
(we all know them)
who burn crosses in the sandpit,
draw stick figures
hanged
in the housing project,
and plan
another picnic rally down the road

what should you do?

DON'T encourage them.
Witness by your absence,
stay away, do not
oppose it do not confront it
leave town for the weekend
but first
come to church, pray
peacefully,
in a spirit of
reconciliation,
for those misguided souls

Yes, we *know* the protesters
will be as last time
Puerto Rican, black and poor,
most of them anyway,
I know too we all
feel for them, we
deplore racial prejudice
everyone is welcome here

even so, they cannot be controlled
there will be blood they are
misled by communists
they strike back
they throw things
they're violent!

which is not our way

Consequently we are taking out
a fullpage ad—
to wash our hands of them
before anything happens,
we'll attack them for being
as bad as the klan

we'll say it loud and clear
the Judeo-Christian tradition
affirms that God wills
for all creation
justice and peace

in this way we can
continue to uphold
for the community
our high moral and spiritual standard

SOUP KITCHEN

Thank God and the many
instruments of God,
for the outpouring
of support
for the Covenant Soup Kitchen.

Statistics tell just
part of the story.
Affects, person-to-person
interactions, joys and pains
do not show up
statistically. However, we do
have numbers to share.

The first day of feeding
56 people were fed.
We averaged almost
60 people that week.

Monday and Thursday
78 and 70 people were fed.

And up to 50 volunteers
complemented
these exciting statistics.

Yes, we have gotten out of the gate
very quickly!
Our beginning estimates were
exceeded, happily
and joyfully!

Before each meal, 12 to 15
nourished their souls
at the altar.

As Isaiah has said:
when we feed the hungry
our light will penetrate
the darkness, our true
joys will be found . . .

Praise the Lord!

Next week we expect
we shall do even better.

THE LAST SUPPER

ROME (UPI) John Paul II marked
the Last Supper of Christ
and his apostles—
washing and kissing the feet
of a dozen
destitute old men
from a home founded
by Mother Teresa of Calcutta

winner of the 1980
Nobel Peace Prize.

*

John Paul, dressed
in white and gold vestments, holding
the golden staff of
St. Peter, sat
on a velvet throne
head bowed, as two priests
read in Latin and Greek
the gospel, recalling
the last night Christ
spent with his apostles
before his crucifixion.

This gesture of humility
was performed
by the pope, who is also
bishop of Rome,
at a mass in the Basilica
of St. John's in Lateran

where 10,000 people were delighted
by John Paul's joining in
singing
with the Vatican choir.

*

Vatican Radio said
the men were chosen
because they represent
'the poorest of the poor.'

*

Easter ceremonies begin
officially
when the pope lights the large
white and gold candle
by the main altar
in St. Peter's, when

angels who waited
with bated breath, heave
skyward
sighs of relief
as Jesus rises from the dead

as John Paul turns over
all
the riches of the church
to the poor

*

who represented

sewers
of beds and cribs,
Calcuttas
picked over
yielding prizes
honors, model poor houses,
miraculous velvet, marble, gold threads
the wealth the church
ripped off

who embodied too
humility
the pope in all
his white and gold power and
glory
expropriated today

kissing and singing

scavenging stripping them clean

NICANOR O NICANOR

So what
let them go to hell
why should they care
whose ass I kiss?
what are they, virgins?
history will absolve me
they made their living
why shouldn't I make mine
you think it's easy, playing polite
at that pay those hours
with a shit eating grin?
let me tell you, I work for mine
history will absolve me
what if nobody *is* left
to talk to, still my books
sell themselves in Santiago
not just downtown but in
the better neighborhoods,
my *OBRA GRUESA*
my boxed
postcard poems under
the noses of police, and
not under the counter either but
published by the Catholic University
history will absolve me
besides
who the hell are you
you thought you could stick it to me
over cocktails you thought
you could drag down my reputation
who gave you the right,
question my ethics
I'll dance on your grave

WORLD AS OYSTER

for Sarah Caldwell
& the Opera Company of Boston

At the First Manila Film Festival

sparing no expense, the First
Lady, Imelda Marcos
in her two-foot diamond necklace,
multicarat diamond teardrop
earrings and highpowered
movie lights, with her husband
the President, presiding at
a medieval pageant of native
dancers, beauty queens and religious
floats bearing bejeweled figures
of the Infant Jesus, and
discoing with George Hamilton
the actor, threw
parties so lavish
guests nibbling from the carcasses
of roasted cows, drinking
$100 bottles of French champagne,
went gaga comparing this
to Hollywood in the 20s,
a Cecil B. DeMille spectacular,
a set for Camelot

surely, as in some
marvelous innocent
old folktale

if shit were gold
Imelda might have been
the perfect asshole

THE
PARTHENON
VERSION

*"Hegel remarks somewhere that all facts
and personages of great importance in
world history occur, as it were, twice. He
forgot to add: the first time as tragedy, the
second as farce . . ."*

—*Marx*

as one of many
grandiose projects
by the First Lady,
the film center
copied from the Parthenon
and built on trash fill
in Manila Bay, was
a last minute decision:

given less than six months
8,000 workers worked
24 hours a day, right up
to the gala opening

though midway through, it
partly collapsed killing
two dozen workers

and finished off moments
before the guests, cement
dust in the air,
sat on the edge of their seats
all through the ceremonies, to
leave quickly before
the screening of the first film

because by then
the April 6 Movement, or
Freedom Fighters of the Philippines
had warned: bombs
are buried in these walls

and if this is a farce
why isn't anyone laughing?

THE SOVIET UNION INVADES AFGHANISTAN

When the Soviet Union invades Afghanistan, the Soviet Union invades Afghanistan.

When Israel invades Lebanon, Israel does not invade Lebanon. Israel liberates Lebanon. The operation is called Peace for Galilee.

It takes many corpses to make this peace. Many arms, legs, eyes. Arms to be raised or lowered, legs to crouch running, eyes not to see. And it takes many ceasefires. When the Israelis daily declare a ceasefire, all west Beirut scurries for shelter from the bombs and shells that are sure to follow.

Israel liberates Lebanon from armed Palestinian refugees who live near people. Near Lebanese, who live in the way of Israeli bombs. Even nearer their own families, also in the way. This demonstrates Palestinian cynicism: they wrap themselves in their mothers' skirts. Now, to get at Palestinians armed to protect the refugee camps they and their families live in, the Israelis must shell helpless civilians. Why don't the refugees live somewhere else. Why don't they go home? as a midwestern American reporter put it. Why must they live among people?

On Israeli news, Palestinian refugees are terrorists. Not men women babies, farmers, auto mechanics, secretaries, school kids, girls washing clothes, peddlers, nurses, guerrillas. Including, doubtless, some suicide commando terrorists. No, like any epidemic, homeless Palestinians are without exception international terrorists. That's why the Israeli army must imprison their doctors, cutting off water, electricity, food and medical supplies.

Israel harbors no terrorists. Menachem Begin and Ariel Sharon are not international terrorists. They are Prime Minister and Defense Minister, respectively, of the state of Israel. Yitzhak Shamir is the Foreign Minister. They have not gotten where they are, to become respectable, by blowing up hotels or massacring innocent villagers in Qibya, in Deir Yassin and elsewhere.

This very morning, 4 August 1982, Prime Minister Begin announced, to laughter and clapping from 200 visiting Americans come to support the invasion, that soon he'll be offering package tours of Lebanon, that already at the northern Israeli border there's a tourist boom. "Their hotels are one hundred per cent full," he said. "It should only happen to the Waldorf Astoria." Does this sound like international terrorism? He even keeps his word. During the siege of Beirut he sends busloads of tourists to sightsee the new ruins of Sidon.

But before tourists arrive in force, Palestinians must be gotten rid of. Naturally it is not enough to kill them. They must be annihilated philosophically as well. As "two-legged beasts." So as Begin and Sharon pursue this extermination-and-dispersal policy into Beirut and beyond--not counting Palestinians or goats or

shredded orange groves in the death toll, but
invoking god the bible and metaphysical genetic
superiority over common humanity—their banner of
sordid sacred righteousness is raised over the
mortified illusions of those innocents who believed
fascism had to be German or other, and that victims
of racism could not themselves commit racist murder.

For when Israeli soldiers in Sidon methodically beat certain
prisoners to death, tying ankles to wrists behind the
back and lashing the human bundle to a tree, who
was so principled as to ask: if not Nuremburg, where
will the war crimes trials be held after *this* war? and
who will hold them?

In Tel Aviv 70,000 Israelis with the passionate humane
courage of their, our, history protest all this, as
Hasidim too hold back, they will not go along, nor
will the young Colonel Eli Geva who resigns, and
these confirm that history as warm and precious as an
arm an eye a leg

yet even these are left behind as events pass them by—as the
basket of amputated Lebanese and Palestinian limbs
in a basement field hospital under Beirut is also left
behind, arms and legs nameless now with no
nationality whatever, unable to stop the slaughter,
for nothing of this or any historical witness will
kick or wave or make anything happen ever again
as it looks on, horrified.

But what do they behold? How did they understand what
was going on?

For when Begin and Sharon (with their bosses officers and
colonial administrators) hired rightwing Moslem

goon squads and Christian Phalangist gangs
modeled on the Hitler Youth of the 30s, and when
they squeezed patriotic anguish and fear from Israeli
workers, taxing money iron and blood to pay for this,
and shelled not only Palestinian refugee camps but
other wretched working neighborhoods, theirs was
not the army of a chosen people or a master race nor
of the Jews, but the old pitiless army of class war daily
pounding the rubble of the irrepressible poor

including, in time, the pacifists the socialists the trade
unionists and always at the end of the line, now
momentarily confused, the darker impoverished
oriental Jews of Israel, too.

For when that army overruns refugee camps and bulldozes
what shelters are left, it wants the homeless without a
country to be homeless without a roof, a kitchen, a
corner to sleep in. It wants those homeless scattered
across the earth, homeless as flies which it may spray
and swat with cluster bombs and white phosphorus,
whose one command is to cut and burn human flesh.

They do not even eat this flesh. Only destroy, destroy,
destroy: leaving it for anti-semites to feast on, like
maggots, who are the camp followers and secret
agents of General Sharon, Ariel Sharon, the butcher
with the name of god's lioness, of altars, of plains and
Arabian gazelle, who thrusts and lunges from cabinet
meetings to carnage in his body of a lumbering toad.

And the worst is, the ordinary boyish graying Israeli soldier
is not killing flies. From hills and gun emplacements
around the city, he is pounding and crushing his
speck of a brother, a sister, his father mother his own
children, it is his own death he is obeying, holding
his ears, observing it from a distance. The silence is
sickening

as the quest for a final solution is carried on by those who
endured to prove triumphant there is none. For what
have they sacrificed? To make a homeland creating
endless homelessness. Then why are they closing
ranks? To force another diaspora.

Only the names have changed.

SACRED COWS,
TROJAN HORSES

On the heels of President Reagan's whirlwind
visit to Tegucigalpa,
in the searing exhaust of an entourage
of dollars, boy scout sarcasm
freedom and green berets

but before Pope John Paul's scheduled
springtime
procession through Central America, through
the mysterious misery of Central America,
before with his miter and staff
he puts down the menace
of liberation theology

already General Sharon, jouncing, the sack of guts
under his belt slopping over, flies to Honduras
reviews troops from the back of a jeep
he will arm them again
again send advisers, showing
how to cut down, and drown, peasants fleeing El Salvador,
how to raid villages in Nicaragua,
they will leave behind the inedible
heads on poles

now you get the point:
keep your eyes open
a while longer,
now do you see
what they were up to

FROM THE ASHES

"unabashed
socialist-realism propaganda"
the National Endowment for the Humanities
Chairman called it

funny, I'd thought it
a film about Nicaragua,
about ordinary shantytown Nicaraguans
battered by waves of U.S. marines
yet sprouting up, through
the rubble of Somoza's terror,
growing in patches over the wounds
of this 20th century

still the Humanities Chairman
drew the line, "it is political
propaganda, not the humanities"

and to think I'd thought it
a TV film about a shoemaker
his wife
3 daughters 1 son

actually,
there *was* a newspaper owner
who'd opposed Somoza, and
opposed, now, the Sandinista government
from a lawn chair by his swimming pool:
easygoing, liberal, personable

yet weightless, rattled, his words lost on
the large delicate earthen
shoemaker's wife, learning
revolution from her teen-age daughter

because of them and many like them
it's true, Somoza had fled
looting the treasury leaving
Managua in ruins

and it's true
the farmers still had it rough,
there they were
right in front of us
complaining to a Sandinista official
things are no better now
than before, and the official
with a pained look saying
"we're a poor country
we can't turn around
overnight it will take years
maybe 10, 20, 30 . . ."
and neither official nor farmer
was content,
never mind happy,
not to have cheaper seeds

maybe that's what the
Chairman of the National Endowment
meant, saying it was
"not the humanities . . ?"

because the shoemaker's wife
was relieved, yet
crying because

under the revolutionary government
all 3 daughters were sent
up into the hills
among volcanos and lakes
to teach the forgotten the peasants
to read and write

she and her husband even went
by bus, looking for them
beyond even the telephone,
to make sure they were not
as rumor had it
turning against their parents

in fact the girls were homesick
and wept a little
and were proud, older, also
heavier than before

maybe that's why
the Chairman of the Humanities
attacked this for being
one-sided

because meanwhile Somoza's guardsmen
were in prison,
there, on film,
complaining to the warden
(himself a former prisoner in this
prison Somoza built)
of overcrowding in the cells
because under the Sandinista government
no one was executed
nor tortured,
though early on, out of

rage, grief
and rough justice
there must have been beatings,
and guardsmen in the neighborhoods
who should have been, and were, shot

so the Chairman of the National
Endowment for the Humanities
must have felt
humiliated,
because his own agency had
without knowing it
funded this film

in it
Nicaraguan ex-guardsmen
had joined Cubans in Florida training
to invade Nicaragua
in berets stetsons mirror sunglasses

and an elderly lady
by a palm tree in Managua
was saying let them come, we're ready
they may get in but once here
they'll piss their pants

this in the film
that has undermined the
Endowment for the Humanities

was it that old lady
who did the humanities in?

I don't know, but later
the shoemaker's wife the
mother of 3 daughters

and 1 son, said
quietly half to herself
(or was it her daughter
speaking for her mother?)
before the women just had
washing cooking kids
now she said smiling
there were 'other things'
but did not elaborate

a pity she didn't, she
clearly had news for us

because now life was complex
surprising
the whole family talked together
politics ran its probing unbroken
thread through everything . . .
and when the oldest daughter who
was doubtless the vanguard
and listened to patriotic folksongs
criticized her youngest sister
who tuned in to American rock
the youngest said, wait
you were my age once
you had your time
let me have mine

and the brother mediating
said, look
Nicaraguan music is for listening
American music is for dancing

smiling, pleased

they all smiled, for
that was that

and all this had started
one day
before the revolution, when
the oldest daughter had come home from school
hiding, for the night, a Sandinista flag
and her father had said, why?
we'll all be killed!
but next day walked her back to school
he carrying the flag
because "if they catch us
it's me they'll kill, not you"

now, on top of that

the same shoemaker and his family
who still live in a shack,
these sweet ingenuous people
their plump cheerful daughters
and shy son
have hit
the enemy where he hurts

that they did this, and were
so nice about it,
I mean, that it was
their decency did it,
is wonderful beyond words

because as good as the film
itself makes us feel,
this last
repercussion, which bonds
those people with us
who struck
our common enemy,
and made him pay for it

this was, is, if anything
even more
heartwarming than the film itself

STATE POWER

This is Horace's story.
He says it beats on him
like a bad dream.

Every saturday he passes
leaflets out, at
the mouth of the subway.

He, and a few others.

With a bullhorn
they speak out against
the dictatorship
of bosses.

And every saturday
a gang of hecklers
threatens them.

One fishfaced kid, especially
vicious, gets to him.

Horace knows he could beat
him and his buddies
into the ground.

The kid knows Horace knows,
and Horace knows
the kid does

because both see
the cop always
there, on the opposite corner,

if Horace makes a move
he'll flash and howl
in a swarm of cops
clubbing Horace to the street.

'So I look at the kid,
he looks at me,
and we both know
what this is all about'

this is Horace speaking.
Which is to say, it is
his gray hair blur,
his round black face,
his candor
and his rage, speaking

it is not a dream.

NOT
ENTIRELY
INNOCENT

for Henrik Nordbrandt

So, you were arrested on a peace march!?

Well, no, it was a march against
a Ku Klux Klan rally.

And the police found guns
that happened to be in your car?

They didn't happen to be there.
We put them there.

To use?

Well, to defend ourselves and others
if it came to that.

Then you weren't entirely innocent!

We had a rifle and a shotgun,
unloaded. Which is legal.

Yes, but, you brought them on purpose.

Of course.

Of course we did, we had
the shells in our pockets.
Yet what would be entirely innocent,
not to show up at all?
Or close the old ponderous doors
to preach to ourselves, and pray?
Or after the Greensboro murders
to have gone like martyrs, knowing
the courts hearing the shots,
seeing bodies fall
again and again on videotape,
would declare their killers innocent?

What morality is it
to roll yourself out under their feet
like a red carpet?

Henrik, we were more innocent then
than you and I are now,
sitting talking here
over a beer and a cigarette.
We were as innocent
as one can be
in these times, this country,
under the present regime

GOLDEN MEAN

They call the rage of the oppressed
extremist.

Evenhanded
censure,
from the hypothetical center of

the slaughter, they call impartial, objective

CRAZY

these bastards are taking my kids
my welfare, she says
where'd they put the jobs,
Fidel wouldn't do that

in one breath says
I want a gun
help!

and in another,
I challenged Reagan
to execute me on TV,
in front of my kids
in person

and you say she's crazy?
OK she's crazy,
now what is sane

FAMILIAR TERMS

The senior undersecretary
explains 'hegemony'
in plain terms, to
people like himself:

take Central America. It's
like looking under the bed.
What you find depends on
how far you want to look.

Take Guatemala. It's like
when your neighbor's party
gets out of hand, you call
the police, or the warden
to silence the barking dog
that's keeping you up.

But
what is he talking about?

The party is guerrilla war.
The cops are
the cops, yet are
the father of the girl
picked up for questioning.
They are more the father
two days later in the morgue
stunned, saying 'but
she wasn't pregnant!'

and more, more
the government death squad
that is the father
lifting up the shroud
who sees her belly slit,
stuffed
with the head of her lover

and the senior undersecretary,
the 45 year old teen-ager
incessantly patting his cowlick
is saying: take El Salvador . . .

what is he talking about!?

on the rocks of El Playón
the dog
is already a headless corpse

WHAT IS POETRY

On 27 July 1982 the Reagan administration certified human
  rights progress in El Salvador. On 27 July 1982 only
  4 mutilated bodies were found dumped in weeds
  by the highway to the barracks of Atlacatl Battalion,
  the elite unit trained by U.S. military advisers
  in weapons, tactics, public relations and sensitivity
  to human rights.

Progress was determined by the fact that fewer victims were
  reported than at this time last year, and none was
  a mother a senior citizen or infant in arms. Three
  were shirtless males, late teens, with rope burns about
  their necks, stab marks in their throats and chins, and
  wire cuts around their thumbs. The fourth, a girl
  who appeared to be about 14 years old, was naked
  except for a piece of bloody clothing at her waist (one
  eye had been gouged out)

WHAT IS POETRY

We know it doesn't rhyme much anymore
but is it beautiful is it true
does it transcend the moment
which moment

or is it ironic, does it echo, echo what
does it have ears

at night whom does it adore
yet at dawn
what dream would it go to the wall for

or is it vituperative, why not
doesn't it express powerful feeling,
an overflow of feeling, is it sincere
is that enough

does it lay bare the soul
or explore the give-and-take of intense personal
                    interrelationships
which persons, what kinds of interrelationships
work or play or
why one and not the others

is it witty, profound, wittily profound, profoundly witty,
is it avant-garde does it shock the bourgeoisie
who love it

or is it above the social arena does it circle the earth,
        a satellite with a proper sense of gravity high
        above the winds of fashion
who put it up there
does it transmit breathtaking pictures of a tiny earth
to a tiny earth
if not, is it a vision of eternity
tell us about it

does it make anything happen
or does it die to itself, till others notice the smell
is it shrill does its voice crack
or must it be a baritone of honey
does it give pleasure, does it teach, delight, uplift
whom does it persuade
whom doesn't it

is it a set of rules a code of forms
what is the principle behind the rules
was it handed down and by whom
or pieced together in a workshop too long ago to remember
can it be rearranged on the shelf
who really cares
may it be dismantled

is it moving, either way moving
is it the imitation of an action
which action

is it a bunch of willy-nilly impressions
who is impressed

if it were a crib
would you trust your baby to sleep in it
bounce up and down in it
learn to stand up in it then
don't answer that

is it a world created by the poet
for the poet of the poet
does it exist for its own sake,
but if it's a way of breathing, whose way
do they smoke are they
breathing making love or getting off work

is it the ideology of a class or the puff of genius
genius for what what class
what are you talking about
is it a man speaking to men
a woman speaking to women
or universal human speaking
to no one in particular
that is, no one at all

is it a mirror held up to nature,
to human nature,
or is it an escape, is it
a mirror held up to nature, to escape human nature, or
a mirror held up to human nature
to escape human history

are you afraid of it
do you understand it

does it embody human values,
values as they are
or as they say they are,
which humans, which values
is it for or against
or does it take no position,
where did it go then
does it levitate, is it in heaven

is it then beyond all this
what is it, where, if you know tell us

but if you don't know
shut up, we'll understand

POE VOTES

Wednesday Oct. 3rd, 1849
all liquored up
and dragged
(Crane guesses)
retching through Baltimore,
polling place to polling place
to Ryan's 4th Ward,
each time a different
dead man, with
his semblance of a life,
and each time
under another name
this same sad man
dying those deaths
became
a whole gang of votes:
this sorry man
jingle man,
this haunting
genius of American letters

DOWN HOME
PRISON POEM

for Luis

We come as friends
with the best intentions

to commiserate,
cheer you up, discuss
lawyers, cases

bandy about
Frankie's latest, confirming
who drinks too much
who seasoned the turtle stew
how good it was,
how Ralph still
talks about a job
as though he really looked

and what guys hang out
still, on the stoop,
catcalling girls
on Main Street

or who skipped town
on charges
to be lost
in New York, New Jersey, Miami

slipping like fish
into a sea of Spanish

we come to go
over this

to tell you
without telling you
in so many words
and yet, without lies,
the great world the
life is passing you by

because all this talk
changes nothing,
nothing

we could be shadows

"WHEN
THE TIME COMES"

When the time comes
I will do
what must be done

he said, and meant it

even as he spoke
the time had come

TKO

In his heart of hearts
his deep dark
metaphysical concept

he concluded
the time had come
and gone

bam! out
like a light,
a halo of black stars . . .

yet even as
he dwelt on this
the time kept

coming and going
coming and going

and in his heart he
felt this,
but did not dare

admit it, not
to himself
not to anyone

WHAT
ARE WE
WAITING FOR

We are waiting for the moment
to make our move

as we did in
fact, in one or another
capital, under dusty palm trees, wait out
splintered bursts of gunfire,
the body of naked rags
bunched-up at a snag in the river

yet this too passed

oranges tumbled into market bins
bottles of milk were stacked in the shade
all by themselves
the children took a bus crosstown to school
someone disappeared
we had another cup of coffee
3 days later we heard
he had been picked up about the time
the kids were coming home from school

what could we have waited for
a solar eclipse? declaration of war?
what was so unusual?

it was just another day

now gone.   You eat
an apple, work out, have
a glass of beer, water the cactus
once in awhile
read a book, vow
to be honest and straightforward
hedging only a little

cheating only
on death, taxes, beauty and, sometimes,
the harder truths

but in how many days
who will tell you
nothing was as it seemed, say
who has been taken away
or maybe a job
possibly yours, or
everyone's Social Security

and that the world we see
we live in
does not (never did) exist

RHODODENDRON

for Arlene

You said, there's a poem in that rhododendron.
I said, not for me.
Elizabeth Bishop, maybe, but she's dead:
tough-minded lady with her cigarette always
smoking, I liked her, we both did,
though she *did* make that racist
sexist remark
about cigar rollers in Tampa.
The words out of her mouth
left her propped at the podium
like a quaint, raspy doll.
I almost felt sorry for her.
She had become a period piece.

Yet to her credit, in its heyday
the flat skeptical voice kept damping down
the pollen dust she kept stirring up.
She picked and praised, yet
with a few colorful exceptions
hardly ever got carried away or lost
in the bug-eyed, detailed, luminous rush
where time broke off

where there was a poem
in the rhododendron

*

But what I meant was not
what Brecht meant, either, asking
what times are these when
talking about trees is almost a crime,
because such talk is so much silence
about so much horror.

How could it be criminal
to speak of trees!

I meant: the horror, or what
that cloud of a word covers up,
has come over
the look in the rhododendron,
has left only
this fleshy leaved bush
of big beautiful flowers

but where's the poetry in that?
where is Elizabeth?

*

(what I remember is
the bright snappy day
the genoa sails popping out
fantastic blues, oranges, reds, slippery greens
leaning and skipping like berserk bloomers

we were flying a kite out over
the shallow scallop waters off Duxbury
hauling, tugging
before the line broke

though the kite was so far away
by then, when the twine
dragging like cable, parted, surprised

we didn't mind, in a way
we were relieved, giddy,
Elizabeth fluttered a little
and was, clearly, pleased)

＊

one day we're caught looking

bumblebees and brass-jacketed flies
poke about heaps
of milk pink fluff

as though the yard were 13 or 14 years old
again, beside itself with its first
floppy corsage

the rhododendron grew so fast!

blossom to blossom
blew, crushed

we're puzzling now the odd
petal in each cluster,
the yellowish thumb smudge
of darker yellower spots

we are watching the sun
grow quietly old

*

trees have something to tell us
we could not tell ourselves

*

Ar, I do thrill to some poems
I mean, the honest that open up
looking right at us,
opening *us* up,
I enjoy the rhododendrons
the pink more than the purple,
they're so fresh
they will never be accomplices,
it's not that I can't feel for this
or for Elizabeth or what
made Brecht cold as leather,
doesn't it get to most people?

but if there's a poem in this
it will have to be
you, saying
(don't ever stop saying it)
there's a poem in the rhododendron

(insist, insist) there's a
poem in it!

James Scully was born in 1937 in New
Haven, CT. Winner of the 1967 Lamont
Award, he was also the recipient of a 1973
Guggenheim Fellowship. He spent
1973-74 in Santiago de Chile, during the
early stages of the Pinochet regime, which
he documented and attacked in his
SANTIAGO POEMS.

also by James Scully

THE MARCHES (Holt, Rinehart & Winston, 1967;
                    reissued 1979 by Ziesing Brothers)
AVENUE OF THE AMERICAS (University of Massachusetts Press, 1971)
SANTIAGO POEMS (Curbstone Press, 1975)
SCRAP BOOK (Ziesing Brothers, 1977)
MAY DAY (Minnesota Review Press, 1980)